10-Session
FAITH-BASED
LEADER'S GUIDE

Copyright
©
2001
by
Doreen L. Hanna

Original Design and Publication
La Semilla Publishing, Los Angeles, CA

2010 Design and Content Update
Kara Ashbaugh & Doreen Hanna

For Information contact
Treasured Celebrations Ministries
www.treasuredcelebrations.org

Dedication and Acknowledgements

2001
To my daughters
Brandy Danielle Corea & Kamy Gay Hanna.
My precious God given gifts that have increased my measure of
faith and brought abundant blessings into my life.
I look forward to all that God has for you, knowing that
"You have been born for such a time as this."

My deepest gratitude to Heather Hershberger and Vetress Arnold
for their enthusiastic encouragement and many hours of
commitment to assist in creating what is within the covers of this
Leader's guide.

My deepest gratitude to my husband Chad
who has been the wind beneath my wings.

2010
To Kara Ashbaugh
You are a treasured gift and blessing to this ministry. Your heart
for women of all ages shows in your passion to create with
excellence what they love - beauty for the eye to behold and
content that speaks to the heart. Your contribution to this
updated project will be embraced by many facilitators that will
soon come to appreciate your God-given gifts! May the Lord bless
you abundantly with His divine favor.

Love from Mom, Wife, and President of TC - Doreen Hanna

TABLE OF CONTENTS

Welcome Leaders!

Throughout this Leaders Guide you will find "Keys to Success" & "Royal Touch" boxes that give you extra helps from facilitators just like you who have already taken groups of ladies through this life-impacting program.

In <u>Keys to Success</u>, you will find extra helps and resources that have already been researched and tested – you just reap the benefits of those who have gone before you!

In <u>A Royal Touch</u>, we offer some "EXTRA" ideas. These are little touches for those who have more time and want to give their program "a touch" more royalty.

Items marked with a CD logo are found on the Supplemental CD available thru Treasured Celebrations (see contact information on title pg.) In the CD, you can find even *more* in depth helps and documents from seasoned facilitators.

For _all_ sessions:
> * Have any handouts copied and ready in advance of class
> * Marking what you will assign as homework each week with a highlighter makes it easier to see the areas where you need to follow-up later!

For _all_ sessions:
* Set up a presentation table with a pretty table-cloth, lit candles, a tiara, and anything else that screams 'Princess'.
* Using supplemental materials that relate to the lesson topic can help you reach specific needs within each group, making each lesson relevant to the personality of your groups and to you!

Printable items of various documents mentioned here are available in the Supplemental CD.

Session 1:

The Princess Within

Session 1: <u>The Princess Within</u>

1) Begin with an "ice breaker" exercise or game.

2) Show the **BMDP** promo video.

3) Distribute journals & review the 10-Session program and explain the objectives of different Sessions, giving examples of how they will be accomplished.

4) Open journals to Session 1 (their pg.1).
   a) You may want to have them read Day 1 on their own time at home if your time together is short; otherwise read it together now.
   b) Have Girls turn to Session 1, Day 2 in journals (their pg 5)
   c) Encourage them by explaining that the personality profile is a fun way to discover how God has uniquely created each Girl with her own individual gifts
   d) Administer the personality profile.

5) Have each Girl share her highest score and show them that the personality "names" are listed on the next page (column 1–Social Butterfly, column 2–Ind.Leader, etc)

6) Review each Girl's strengths & areas for improvement from the next chart (on your pg. 4-5).
   a) Emphasize the strengths and provide encouragement by explaining that the areas for improvement enable us to see where we need the Lord's help.
   b) Stress that everyone needs improvement in some area.

7) Read and discuss Psalm 139:1-16. (Journal Day 3 - pg 10) Identify phrases that reflect how intimately the Lord knows and loves each Girl.

   a) Explain that they will select one verse from Psalm 139 and write it into their journal in the space provided on pg 11.

   b) Instruct them to meditate daily on the selected verse and to place it in their hearts like "a treasured possession."

8) Explain that Day 4's project in their journal is to obtain input from adult family members or friends about a personality or character trait they admire in them.

   a) Advise each Girl that she will be given three envelopes containing: a note card, a matching envelope, and instructions for completion.*

   b) Encourage them to give one note card to each of three adult family members, teachers, or friends that they love and/or respect.

   c) Remind them that they are to ask each individual to complete one card and return it to them <u>sealed</u> within two or three days. This will allow the Girls to bring them to class the next week.

9) Be sure you have looked at Day 5 of the journal - pg 13.
Knowing your girls - decide if they will do the Mom and Mentor moment each week with their mothers (preferably), with you, or with another mentor or family member.

As each girl shares the results of their Personality Profile, I take notes on a bio sheet that I have the girls fill out first thing! This helps me get to know each of them more quickly and remember who has what personality. I learn their strengths, & weaknesses, too! Later, I can comment when another discussion affirms one of these traits in a princess – and helps when I am introducing each of them during their Celebration.

*For <u>all</u> sessions:
  * Have any handouts copied and ready in advance of class
  * Marking what you will assign as homework each week with a highlighter makes it easier to see the areas where you need to follow-up later!*

* INSTRUCTIONS FOR COMPLETING THE NOTE CARDS:
(You may photo copy this message or use the Supplemental CD
  to print it.)

The young lady from whom you have received this
envelope is participating in a class entitled *"Becoming A
Modern Day Princess."*

Please take a moment to write about one personality or
character trait you love about her on the enclosed note card.
Then sign the card and return it to her within the next two
days in the envelope provided.
Make sure the envelope is <u>sealed</u>.
Next week she will return to class with this sealed note card
and others she has obtained. At that time, she will open all
her sealed envelopes and share what others love about her.

Thank you for your cooperation in helping this young lady
to see a godly characteristic that He has placed within her.

Directions: Read each statement carefully, and then check the one in each <u>row</u> <u>across</u> that most often applies to you. If two apply equally, you may check both.

*Princess Personality Profile

1	2	3	4
I love to tell funny stories. ☐	When I am joking, sometimes people think I'm serious. ☐	I love to laugh, but not when it hurts someone's feelings. ☐	I can keep a straight face when being funny. ☐
I make quick decisions. ☐	I make decisions that are usually right. ☐	I make decisions based on all the facts. ☐	I don't like making decisions. Others can. ☐
I like lots of friends and being the center of attention. ☐	I like being the head of the group. ☐	I like being alone. ☐	I like to go with the flow. ☐
I like to talk a lot rather than listen. ☐	When I talk, people usually listen. ☐	I think carefully before I talk. ☐	I like to listen more than talk. Keeps me out of trouble. ☐
I'm very sociable and make tons of friends easily. ☐	I like to be in charge when I'm with my friends. ☐	I love having a few friends I know really well. ☐	I love to sit back and watch. I'm the quiet one in the group. ☐
I love excitement and change. I get bored easily. ☐	I like a good challenge. ☐	I like schedules and routines. ☐	I like variety. Knowing a little bit about a lot of things. ☐
I try to make everything fun. ☐	I get things done quickly and efficiently. ☐	I think and plan before I do something. ☐	I do things to be helpful and please others. ☐
If I were stranded on an island . . . I'd look for other people. ☐	If I were stranded on an island . . . I'd figure out how to get us rescued. ☐	If I were stranded on an island . . . I'd explore it. ☐	If I were stranded on an island . . . I'd relax and enjoy the beach. ☐
Total _____	Total _____	Total _____	Total _____

Total each column above

Apply the totals from each column on the personality profile to the corresponding columns below:

Knowing Me—My Strengths and Weaknesses

Social Butterfly	INDEPENDENT LEADER	Organizational Queen	Dependable Friend
Strengths	**Strengths**	**Strengths**	**Strengths**
• Loves to talk	• Born leader	• Organized	• Great listener
• Expressive	• Loves to take charge	• Analytical	• Well liked
• Bubbly	• Independent	• Sensitive and thoughtful	• Quiet
• Funny	• Self-sufficient	• Has high standards	• Patient
• Good storyteller	• Dynamic	• Appreciates beauty	• Calm, cool, and collected
• Lives in the moment	• Active	• Creative/ Artistic	• Dry sense of humor
• Enjoys people	• Is usually right	• Musical	• Sympathetic and kind
• Creative	• Excels in emergencies	• Conscientious	• Easy to get along with
• Energetic	• Confident	• Likes schedules	• Dependable
• Volunteers	• Quick worker	• Detailed	• Consistent
• Inspires others	• Likes to set goals	• Needs to finish things	• Peacemaker
Weaknesses	**Weaknesses**	**Weaknesses**	**Weaknesses**
• Forgetful	• Too controlling	• Easily depressed	• Stubborn
• Tends to exaggerate	• Insensitive	• Too sensitive	• Not enough enthusiasm
• Doesn't like being serious	• Impatient	• Dwells on negatives	• Compromises too often
• Gullible and naive	• Perceived as unfeeling	• Perfectionist	• Indecisive
• Disorganized	• Doesn't like to share credit	• Skeptical of others' motives	• Lacks energy
• Leaves things unfinished	• Too focused, can't relax	• Stresses over details	• Takes the easy way out

Social Butterfly	INDEPENDENT LEADER	Organizational Queen	Dependable Friend
I love . . .	**I love . . .**	**I love . . .**	**I love . . .**
• Attention • Affection • Approval • Acceptance	• Supportive people • Being appreciated • Abilities recognized • Goals achieved	• Stability • Space • Silence • Sensitively	• Peace and quiet • Respect • Being valued • Emotional support
I hate . . .	**I hate . . .**	**I hate . . .**	**I hate . . .**
• Budgets • Deadlines • Schedules • Criticism • Boredom • "Stick in the mud's"	• Messed up schedules • Unproductive work • Laziness • Disloyalty • Not being appreciated • No independence	• Making a mistake • Being mis-understood • Compromising • Forgetfulness • Being late • Disorganization	• Conflict • Change • Pushy people • Loud music or talking • People who think I'm not smart because I'm quiet
I offer . . .	**I offer . . .**	**I offer . . .**	**I offer . . .**
• Colorful creativity • Optimism • Entertainment • A light touch	• Good time management • Good judgment • Fresh perspective • Strong work ethic	• Sense of detail • A love of analysis • Great follow-through • High standards	• Peacemaking skills • Objectivity • Problem-solving skills • A shoulder to cry on

Leader's Notes:

Session 2:
A Royal Destiny

Session 2 : *A Royal Destiny*

A Royal Touch

> *On your presentation table, display pictures, mementos scrapbooks, etc., that represent your family &/or heritage.*

Keys to Success

> *Be sure to affirm each young lady as she finishes reading her cards – especially when a card affirms a Personality Profile discoveries from last week.*

A Royal Touch

> *When the girls finish reading their cards, provide a way to preserve and protect them:*
> *- attach each one in their journals by stapling onto the back cover*
> *- provide a special pocket folder to hold extra papers, handouts, etc., and attach the cards there.*
> *(see * "A Royal Touch: as a special gift" on page 8)*

1) Have each Girl open her envelopes and share aloud what others love about her.
   - Emphasize that often others see in us character traits that we don't see in ourselves. This is one way God speaks to and encourages us through others.

2) Have each Girl place her note cards in her journal after reading them.
   - Remind them to periodically review the comments as a means of providing encouragement whenever "they don't *feel* loved."

3) Have each share the verse from Psalm 139 that she selected as her "treasured possession."(journal pg 11)
   - Briefly discuss and affirm their choices.

4) Stress to your group that anything shared in your discussions together should always be considered private and confidential, and should never be shared with someone outside the class setting.

5) Begin this Session's topic with examples of a family heritage using the provided summaries or other key verses.
   - <u>Esther 2 – Esther 8.</u>
   For you: God's people were preserved through Esther. Esther was Jewish. She was chosen from her people who were in slavery to King Ahasuerus, to be in his harem. Haman, an officer of the king, sent out a decree that dictated all the Jews be killed. Esther's uncle, Mordecai, asked her to go to the king to implore his favor and plead with him for her people. Her obedience to God, by obeying Mordecai and Hegai, gave her favor with the king. By gaining the king's favor, Esther was able to save the Jewish nation. (A more detailed paraphrased summary of the story of Esther is provided at the end of this chapter.)

6) In journals, turn to pg. 18. Define 'heritage' & 'legacy': have the Girls read the definitions!

Discussion questions:
- What were some of the positive qualities of Esther's heritage and/or legacy?
- What parts of her heritage could have held her back?
- Did Esther do this alone? Whose help did she ask for?
- Was Esther obedient? To whom?
- What were her rewards for being obedient?

Esther's heritage and upbringing, along with her God-given destiny, placed her in a position to save a **whole nation.** <u>**You**</u> **were created with a legacy and destiny as well – and just like Esther, you were created "for such a time as this".**

- When you are in trouble, what or whom do you call on to help you so you aren't alone?
- What rewards have you seen when you have been obedient?
- What does your journal say Esther's name means? Do you know the meaning of your name?

7) Provide an example of your own family heritage.
   - Emphasize that there are different kinds of inheritances. Some examples include godly people, financial, fame and fortune, acts of goodness, etc.
8) Prepare the Girls for this weeks' projects:
   a) Turn in journals to Day 2 -pg 19 thru Day 5 -pg 24 and review the research they will be doing to discover their family tree and heritage. Day 5 should be done with their mother or a female member of their family if possible.
   b) Encourage them to bring back these discoveries next week to share in class.

Give them this verse to meditate on this week:
<u>*Psalm 16:6 (paraphrased)*</u>
"The family line has been passed on to me.
Indeed, my heritage is beautiful to me."

Another question for discussion: "Is there a specific time in history you have always wished you had been born in? Do you think that the time you live in is vital to your destiny?"

Keys to Success

Point out that: "Your Heritage helps create your destiny, but it does NOT rule it!" We learn about our heritage so that we can chose to either embrace it or learn from it - portions we want to change... Most families <u>do</u> have something negative in their histories, but these are just as are valuable to know – they help us begin to understand why our families function the way they do.

The girl's journal offers a blank family tree chart that they can fill in with information they glean from interviewing family

CD

A Royal Touch

As special gifts, I have put each Princess's name and its meaning – sometimes with their main Personality Trait included, too - on a bookmark, in a picture frame, or mounted on a <u>pocket folder</u> to hold extra paper, handouts, and their affirmation cards.

CD

Optional - not in girl's journal:

<u>Read 2 Timothy:1-5</u>
Eunice was a woman who took the responsibility of teaching God's Word to her son Timothy. This teaching made him "wise through faith." (2 Timothy:3-15) When Timothy was still young, Eunice's husband died leaving her to raise her son with the help of her mother.

Two factors molded Timothy's life:

- His godly mother Eunice and faithful grandmother Lois touched his life from early childhood. By teaching him the Word of God, they prepared him for God's call to salvation and ministry.
- Hearing the gospel again later, as an adult, through Paul, and being mentored by him.

The legacy Timothy's mother and grandmother gave was living their lives by what they believed in, thus reflecting a <u>true faith</u>. Paul affirmed that Timothy had that same true faith. This brought great joy to Paul. Timothy's mother and grandmother's faithfulness to God's Word, kept by the Holy Spirit, caused Timothy not to waiver in his faith.

Paraphrased Story of Esther

Esther was a young woman who had been adopted by her Uncle Mordecai because her mother and father had died, possibly during the capture of the Jews by the King of Persia, in whose kingdom the Jews were now enslaved.

During this time of captivity a command went out among the kingdom to gather beautiful young women for the King. The Bible says that Esther was very beautiful; therefore, Esther was chosen along with many other young women to be taken into the care of a man named Hegai, who was to prepare them to be seen by the King.

Esther found favor with Hegai and he provided the best for her beauty preparations. He even moved her, and the maidservants he had given her, to the best place in the house where all the women lived that were being prepared for the King. These women spent 12 months in preparation before they saw the King, being saturated with oils and perfumes. Each woman was then called into the King and, after having been with the King, if he was delighted with her she could come and see him again but only if he called her by name.

Esther was obedient to all of Hegai's advice and she obtained favor in the sight of all who saw her. When she was taken to the King in his royal palace, the King loved Esther more than all the other women and she obtained his grace and favor. The king even had a banquet in Esther's honor and crowned her queen. But she kept it a secret that she was a Jew.

Now Haman, the King's closest advisor, loved his power and it had been decreed by the King that those in his presence should pay him homage. One day Haman became angry because whenever he passed by Mordecai, he would not bow to him – Mordecai only served the God of Israel, the one true God. In his anger he went to the King and asked, "Can I destroy those who are not honoring the king's law ?" The king gave his permission because Haman promised to put money into the King's treasuries for allowing him to do this.

When the decree went out to the kingdom, all the Jews were in great mourning because they knew that they would all be killed. When Mordecai learned of what had happened, he went in front of the king's gate and wept bitterly. Esther heard Mordecai's wails of grief, so she sent one of her servants to speak to him and find out why he was weeping. The servant

returned to show Esther a copy of the decree that Mordecai had sent back to her, clearly stating that the Jews were to be destroyed.

Mordecai also sent a message to Esther saying that she should go to the king and plead for the life of her people. Esther sent a message back to Mordecai that said "no one goes into the inner court to the king who has not been called by name, or they will be put to death, except if the king holds out the golden scepter, then they will live. And, I have not been called to go to see the king for 30 days!"

Mordecai sent back his reply, telling Esther, "Do not think in your heart that you will escape because you are in the King's palace. You are a Jew. If you remain silent at this time, deliverance will arise for the Jews from another place, and you may perish. Yet who knows, it may be that you have come to royalty for such a time as this?"

Then Esther replied again to Mordecai. "Gather the Jews and fast for me for three days. My maids and I will fast likewise. Then I will go to the king, which is against the law, and if I perish, I perish." So, on the third day of fasting Esther put on her royal robes and courageously went and stood in the inner court of the King's palace while the King sat on his royal throne. When the King saw Queen Esther the king held out the golden scepter and Esther went to the King.

The King asked "Whatever you wish, it shall be given to you – up to half of the kingdom." Esther answered, "If it please the King, let the King and Haman come today to a banquet that I have prepared for you." The King quickly accepted and he and Haman joined Esther that evening.

The next day Esther invited the King and Haman to another banquet. Haman went out joyful, but was angry when he saw Mordecai at the king's gate. But he thought to himself, "Queen Esther invited no one but me and the King to the banquet, yet nothing satisfies me until as long as Mordecai is alive."

That night the King could not sleep and asked to read the kingdom Chronicles. As they were read it was found written how Mordecai had told of the attempted murder of the King. The King said "What honor or dignity has been bestowed on Mordecai for this? The King's servants said, "Nothing has been done for him." So the King called Haman in and asked him, "What shall be done for the man whom the king delights to honor?" Haman thought in his heart, "Whom would the king want to honor more than me?" He then answered the King and said, "Let him wear a royal robe, ride the royal horse that only the King has ridden and place a crown upon his head. Then parade him on horseback though the city square and proclaim, 'This shall be done to men whom the King delights to honor.' "

Then the King said to Haman "Hurry, take the robe and horse as you have suggested and do so for Mordecai the Jew. Leave nothing undone of all that you have spoken!" Haman obeyed the King and then hurried to home, humiliated and angry.

A little later that day Haman was at the banquet again with Esther and the King, and after the great meal the King asked Esther, "What is your petition Queen Esther? It shall be granted you." Then Esther answered and said, "If I have found favor in your sight, O king, let my life and the lives of my people be saved. For we have been sold for slavery and now are to be killed. If we were only to be sold as slaves, perhaps I could remain quiet, but even that would bring damage to the reputation of the King."

The King asked, "Who has devised this plan?"

"Haman is the enemy," Esther replied. At that moment one of the king's aides came and said, "Sire, Haman has ordered a 75-foot gallows to be built to hang Mordecai, the man who saved the King from assassination. It stands in Haman's courtyard."

"Hang Haman on it!" the King ordered, and so they did. Then the King gave Haman's estate to Esther and gave his ring to Mordecai, appointing him Prime Minister. He also reversed Haman's order to destroy the Jews.

So that day all the Jews were filled with joy and had a great celebration! And from that day forth it became a tradition that on that day they would celebrate as a remembrance of the time of their fasting and God's answer to their prayers.

Session 3:
The Wealth of Wisdom

Session 3 : <u>The Wealth of Wisdom</u>

A Royal Touch

* Bring several examples of 'rewards' of obedience (i.e. chart w/ gold stars, stickers or homework pass that a teacher might give, report card, a paycheck, a drivers license) Use before the Story of Ruth to introduce today's topic.
* I have a picture of my great-grandmother, grandma, and mother that I put on my presentation table for today.

Keys to Success

Emphasize that peace in your life and with God is the best reward you can have.

Keys to Success

Use the Mom's Quiz to help each daughter get to know her mother better.

1) Have each Girl share about her family heritage discoveries.

2) Begin this Session's topic with the Story of Ruth – This is on Day 4, pg 32 of their journals (yours – pg13) Have the girls take turns reading the story and encourage them to make note of the rewards Ruth experienced in each section. (Example: Paragraph 5- favor; 6-God's blessing; 7-provision & abundance; 9-love & protection; 10- respect; End-a great heritage! She was a great-grandmother to Jesus!)

For you: Ruth chose to go with her mother-in-law Naomi because she must have seen in her that her God was the true God. Ruth sacrificed going home to her own family to be with Naomi. Ruth gleaned the fields and slept at Boaz' feet. Boaz protected Ruth because of her obedience to Naomi. He provided food for Ruth and Naomi and then married Ruth. Ruth became the great-great grandmother of King David, and became part of the lineage of Jesus. (A more detailed summary of the story of Ruth is provided at the end of this chapter.)

3) Discuss the following questions about Ruth:
Why do you think Ruth chose to go with Naomi?
What did Ruth give up by going with Naomi?
Who respected Ruth for her obedience?

From journal:
- Give some examples of where Ruth humbled herself choosing to use wisdom and obey Naomi and others?
- What were Ruth's rewards for being obedient?

4) Discuss the following questions about parents:
a) Do you find it sometimes difficult to obey your parents? Why?

b) Do you believe your parents give you good advice?

c) To whom or where do you go when you don't want to talk with your parents?

5) Discuss the following questions specifically about mothers or the significant women in their lives:

a) What is one thing you love most about her?

b) What have you done lately to let her know you love her?

c) Do you pray for your mother?

6) Prepare the Girls for the project on Day 4. Providing a note card, give them the following instructions:

a) Instruct them to write a note to their mother telling her what they love and appreciate about her.

b) Encourage them to surprise their Mom by placing the note in a location where she would least expect to find such a loving, little gift.

c) Encourage the Girls to persuade their mothers to have a "Mom's Night Out." This could be as simple as going out for a walk or getting ice cream together. The goal is to make this special for Mom.

7) Emphasize the importance of completing the rest following verse to meditate on this week.

Keys to Success

Because details aren't always complete before a program starts, this is a good time to send out an email &/or note to the parents, including:
- unpaid balance on their account
- date for MakeUp & Manners dinner (if not during regular scheduled class times)
- date of Celebration (remind them to contact the man who they hope will bless them & be sure date is good for him)
- areas where you still need help or volunteers (in Celebration or class-times)
- upcoming community service projects (if you ask your girls to do community service during their program)

Proverbs 3:13, 15
"Blessed is the [person] who finds wisdom....
She [wisdom] is more precious than rubies;
nothing you desire can compare with her."

Important Note: Set a date for the parent's meeting regarding preparations for the "Night of Celebration" & let parents know how important it is to attend! (See the end of next session for list of items to prepare &/or *"Make It Your Own"* folder of the Supplemental CD)

The Paraphrased Story of Ruth

There was a couple who lived in Moab and had two sons. Both the sons married and their wives names were Orpah and Ruth. After a period of time, Naomi's husband and her two sons died. After their deaths, Naomi began to encourage Orpah and Ruth to return to the city of their own parents instead of going with her to her hometown. "Maybe there you will be able to marry again," she told them. After continued encouragement Orpah kissed Naomi good-bye and returned to her childhood home, but Ruth insisted on staying with Naomi.

Ruth said, "Don't make me leave you. For I want to go wherever you go and live wherever you live. Your people will be my people and your God my God. May the Lord punish me if I allow anything but death to separate us." When Naomi saw that Ruth had made up her mind, they both made their way to Bethlehem, Naomi's hometown.

When they arrived in Bethlehem Ruth said to Naomi, "Perhaps I can go out into the fields of some kind man and glean the field behind his reapers." Naomi gave her approval, so Ruth did so. As it happened, unbeknownst to Ruth, the field she found herself in belonged to Boaz, a very wealthy relative of Naomi's.

Boaz saw Ruth gleaning one day and spoke to her. "Please stay right here with us to glean the fields, stay behind my women workers. I have warned the young men not to bother you. When you are thirsty, go and help yourself to the water." Ruth thanked him warmly and asked, "How can you be so kind to me, you must know I am just a foreigner?"

"Yes, I know," Boaz replied, "and I also know about the love and kindness you have shown your mother-in-law since the death of your husband. May the Lord bless you for it."

When Ruth returned home she found that she had gleaned nearly a whole bushel. Naomi exclaimed, "Where in the world did you glean today? Praise the Lord for whoever was so kind to you." "I was in the field of Boaz," said Ruth. "Why, that man is one of our closest relatives," cried Naomi excitedly. Ruth than told her all that Boaz had said. Naomi then told her, "Do as he has said."

One day Naomi said to Ruth, "I would love to see you marry Boaz! He has been so kind to us. Now do what I tell you. Take a bath, put on some perfume and some nice clothes, and after dark notice where he lies down to sleep. Then go lie at his feet and he will tell you what to do concerning marriage." Ruth was obedient, replying, "All right. I'll do whatever you say."

She went down to the threshing floor and saw that Boaz had finished his meal and had gone to sleep by a heap of grain. Ruth came quietly and lifted the covering off his feet and lay there. Around midnight, he awakened and sat up. "Who are you?" he demanded.
"It is I sir, Ruth," she replied. "Please make me your wife according to God's law."

Boaz honored the Jewish tradition that allowed a close relative of Naomi to take Ruth as a wife. All other relatives had declined, so Boaz was able to marry Ruth with all integrity. He gave her a son and named him Obed, who became the grandfather of King David.

Leader's Notes:

Session 4:

The Value of True Friends

Session 4 : <u>The Value of True Friends</u>

A Royal Touch

On your presentation table for today's session place a gift or picture that brings back great memories of friendships you have had in your life. Or, have one of your BFFs' come and share about your friendship!

Keys to Success

Have the girls share the qualities they desire in a friend -writing them on a whiteboard. Encourage them to copy the list in their journal. In closing ask them to look at the list again and rate <u>themselves</u> using those same qualities:

"What kind of friend are <u>YOU?</u>"

(this exercise is on Day 2, pg 40 of the girl's journal)

1) Have each Girl share on her discoveries from her study and journals over the last Session. Report on her date with her Mom or mentor.

2) Discuss the following questions for the topic of the Session:
   a) How do you make friends?
   b) What qualities do you value in a friendship?
   c) What makes having friends in your life important?
   d) Where do you go and what do you do when a friend disappoints you?
   e) Why will it be important to have friends in your future?

3) Have the girls turn to Session 4, Day 1 - pg37 in their journals. Read the summary of Luke 1 & 2 – the story of Mary and Elizabeth (your paraphrased summary follows in this chapter).

   Discuss the following questions:
   a) Who was the first person Mary wanted to see after her experience with the angel?
   b) How did Elizabeth receive Mary? Was it with kindness or jealousy?
   c) Do you think they shared their most cherished secrets?
   d) What does that tell us about their relationship?
   e) What does that say about their relationship with God?

4) Prepare the Girls for the journal projects this Session.
   a) Briefly go over each Day in their journal.

b) Provide one or two "friend" cards for them to do the project listed on Day 3 - pg 41 of journal)

c) Encourage them to follow thru with one of the special suggestions listed to do with their friend(s).

d) Refer to pages 42-43 in the BMDP journal to encourage the girls to complete the friend evaluations there.

5) Emphasize the importance of meditating on this verse for the week.

If you want to go Even deeper, use the Friends hip Goals and Respect (in Special Helps on CD)sheet for a more in depth look at the friendships they have.

Romans 13:9 (Living Bible paraphrased)

"...pay all your debts except the debt of love for others, never finish paying that!"

Note: Prepare agenda for the parents' meeting regarding the "Night of Celebration"

See the *"Make It Your Own"* section of the **Supplemental CD**:
- Request for Help
- Imparting a Blessing
- My Favorites Sheet by each daughter

Make sure you have extra copies of all necessary forms

The Story of Mary and Elizabeth

Zacharias and his wife Elizabeth were members of the Levite tribe, and both of them served in the temple of the Lord because Elizabeth had no children. Zacharias and Elizabeth were godly people, careful to obey all of God's laws both in the way they lived and in their hearts.

Elisabeth was barren for a long time. But, one day an angel came to Zacharias and said the God had heard his prayer and that his wife Elizabeth would bear him a son. Soon after this she became pregnant.

Within a few months God sent the angel Gabriel to Nazareth to speak to Mary, a girl who was still a virgin and engaged to be married to a man named Joseph, a descendant of King David. Gabriel appeared to Mary and said, "Congratulations, you are favored by the Lord. Don't be frightened, for God has decided to bless you wonderfully. Soon, you will become pregnant and have a baby boy, and you are to name him 'Jesus.'"

Mary asked, "But how can I have a baby? I am a virgin." The angel replied, "The Holy Spirit shall come upon and the power of God shall overshadow you. Furthermore, six months ago, your Aunt Elizabeth became pregnant in her old age. Remember, every promise from God is true."

Mary said, "I am the Lord's servant, and I am willing to do whatever he wants. May everything you said come true." Then the angel disappeared.

Hearing of Elizabeth's news that she too was pregnant, Mary hurried to visit her. When she arrived Elizabeth exclaimed, "You are favored by God above all other women, and your child is destined for God's highest praise. What an honor this is, that the mother of my Lord should visit me! Mary, you believed that God would do what he said, and that is why he has given you this wonderful blessing."

Mary responded, "Oh, how I delight in the Lord. He took notice of a lowly servant girl and now generation after generation shall call me blessed of God. He has done great things to me." Mary stayed with Elizabeth about three months and then went back home.

Leader's Notes:

Session 5:

Beyond My Kindgom

Session 5 : <u>Beyond My Kingdom</u>

A simple Presentation Table with a cloth, tiara, lit candles, and a Bible is sometimes all that's needed to create an intimate setting for this class. Another idea might include text books, something that represents wisdom, or names &/or pictures of older members of your community who would make good mentors.

Add a quick discussion of what each girl things she is called to do in her future ... a "what do you want to be when you grow up" question. The things they have learned about their personalities, strengths, weaknesses, gifts, talents, & interests so far give you a great spring board to help them see that these things are all "map-points" that God gives to help us see what we are called to do or be. Then the discussion questions can help them think of things they might want to learn about that follow this train of thought...

1) Have each Girl report on her journal activity and project from last Session.

2) Have each Girl pay a compliment to someone in the class to whom she has not already spoken a kind word. The rewards of this exercise cannot be underestimated!

3) Discuss the following questions:
   a) What is one thing you know a lot about?
   b) When did you begin learning about this?
   c) Who helped you gain this knowledge?
   d) Where did you learn these things? (e.g., home, school, church)
   e) Why were you advised or why did you pursue these?
   f) How will this knowledge impact your future?
   g) Why is the knowledge of God's Word important?

4) Turn to Day 3 of Chapter 5. Read Pro. 2:1-10 and allow time to answer questions together or on their own.

Note: This is the time to determine clearly if each Girl has a true understanding and knowledge of her relationship with Christ. If there is any doubt regarding her salvation, provide an opportunity for her to pray and invite Christ into her heart.

5) Prepare the Girls for the journal projects by looking thru pages 45 - 51 in their journals. Briefly review each Day and what they will be doing.

6) Go over Day 5 on pg 51 and stress considering the possibility of a mentor to help them pursue a specific topic they thought about during this study.

7) Emphasize the importance of meditating on the verse of the week (below)or their selected verse from the
Prov. 2:1-10 exercise at the bottom of pg 48 in their journals.

Proverbs 1:7
"The fear of the Lord is the beginning of knowledge."

For __all__ sessions:
   * *Have any handouts copied and ready in advance of class*
   * *Marking what you will assign as homework each week with a highlighter makes it easier to see the areas where you need to follow-up later!*

Leader's Notes:

Session 6:

Looking & Acting

Like a Princess

Session 6 : <u>Looking and Acting Like a Princess</u>

Keys to Success

Often this session is scheduled as a special evening event, and can be used the same week or day as another session. It can be implemented at a restaurant in a special event room, a private home, or as a catered event in your regular room -decorated and set as a fine restaurant. The makeup session is usually first and the meal follows.

A Royal Touch

Sometimes we make this an extra special event by including a movie ("Princess Diaries I or II", The Story of Esther", etc) between the makeup session and the etiquette meal. During the movie, you can speak with each girl individually, checking to see if they are keeping up in their journals, confirming who will be speaking their blessing – and that her father or step-in-dad knows when and where the Celebration will be. This is such a great opportunity to see their hearts.

Note: This is an excellent break in the class structure. It is best to focus on general concepts rather than specifics:

- For make-up, using light colors vs. dark to make features stand out or recede rather than choosing specific shades; work with the shape of your face; use make-up appropriately; hair color vs. skin color, etc.

- For manners, making people feel comfortable and how not to offend unwittingly rather than specific rules

- In general, incorporate Biblical principles of modesty and beauty

1) Review the journal entries made regarding the things they want to pursue *"beyond their kingdom"*. Are they seeking out mentors? What new things are they pursuing?

2) Read Day 1 of Chapter 6 on pgs 53-54
   - What is beauty to you?
   - Think of someone you consider beautiful. What's beautiful about her?
   - Read Proverbs 11:22 and Matthew 2327. From these verses, how do you think God defines beauty?

3) Bring in some mentors! A beauty consultant &/or an etiquette instructor - This could be the same person, two different people, or yourself and someone new. Allow a minimum of 2 to 3 hours for this activity.
   a) Have the beauty consultant give a "natural look" make-over. Focus on **techniques** rather than a specific product line.

b) Have the etiquette instructor share tips on manners, clothing and examples of table settings. Be creative. Provide an opportunity to observe other godly women.

c) Arrange to dine together as you present etiquette tips and instruction.

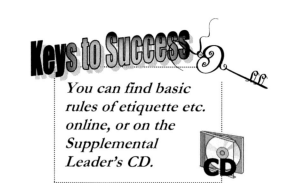

Keys to Success

You can find basic rules of etiquette etc. online, or on the Supplemental Leader's CD.

4) Encourage the Girls to write in the appropriate pages of their journal helpful tips they might want to remember during the beauty **and** etiquette times.

5) Stress the importance of taking care of our physical bodies – pages 55-58 of journal. Beauty starts with good physical health!!

6) Be sure to include appropriate dress during this time together! Many young ladies these days don't give much thought to how the way they dress affects those around them. (Pages 59-61 of journal)

7) Instruct the Girls to set aside time this week to make a list with their parents of the people they want to invite to their "Night of Celebration."
   - Advise them that you will need to know the number of invitations they will need by **next week** to have time to prepare them.

8) Each girl should also complete her **Favorites' Sheet** this week to give to the man speaking her blessing for her night of Celebration

9) Emphasize the importance of meditating on the verse of the week:

1 Peter 3:3-4
"Cultivate inner beauty, the gentle, gracious kind that God delights in."

A Royal Touch

As your girls are finishing their makeup -Take pictures!
This is a perfect opportunity to talk about <u>receiving</u> compliments. (i.e. don't argue, disagree, or refuse a compliment, say" Thank You!") Ask one young lady to compliment one of their fellow Princesses – asking the girl who receives the compliment to give one to someone else until everyone has had a turn to practice both giving AND receiving.

Collect the "My Favorites" worksheet as they are completed (or take the journals and photocopy that page, making TWO copies, so they can keep their original in their journals). You will want to keep one copy in your possession and give/send one to each father. (Often, a girl will lose her copy if it's removed from her journal – or her father will misplace it – leaving you with a crisis on your hands just before a Celebration!)

CD

You should have a Parent's Meeting scheduled for this week to cover the Celebration plans and responsibilities (you can do this before the program starts, if you prefer).

Don't try to do this alone! (The girls will need your attention on their Celebration day/night – keeping nerves to a minimum and solving last minute problems.) Having the parent's help makes it more valuable for the families involved and gives them ownership – and keeps you from overextending yourself!

Leader's Notes:

Session 7:

The Portrait of

A Prince

Provide a copy of the Dad's Quiz to help them go a little deeper with their conversations during the one-on-one time this week with the man who will bless them

1) Have each Girl report on her time with her father or other respected man in her life.

2) Discuss the following questions for the topic of the Session:
   a) Who is the most important man in your life? Why?
   b) What do you love and appreciate about him?
   c) Does he provide encouragement and guidance in your life? How?
   d) How has he influenced decisions you make?
   e) To whom do you go if he isn't available?

3) Read Psalm 15 (Living Bible). This is on Day 1 of Chapter 7 in the journal.

4) Discuss how this scripture describes the qualities of a "Man of Integrity." Page 66 of their journal lists the acronym 'INTEGRITY'. Here is an example of how they might complete it:
   - **I - <u>Invites quality people into his life</u>**
   - **N - <u>Never Slanders or Gossips</u>** (insults, slurs, or smears someone's reputation)
   - **T - <u>Trustworthy</u>**
   - **E - <u>Even Tempered</u>**
   - **G - <u>Generous to others</u>**
   - **R - <u>Respectful towards authority & women</u>**
   - **I - <u>Insightful</u>** (can see potential rewards & consequences)
   - **T - <u>Thankful</u>**
   - **Y - <u>Young at Heart</u>** (enjoys having fun)

5) Discuss how the Girls would compare the qualities of a good future husband to those they admire in their father or other godly men in their lives. See Day 2, page 67 of journal.

6) Prepare the Girl's for the projects in their journals this week.
   a) Review Days 3 thru 5, talking encouraging them to complete each activity.
      - Day 3 may bring up some big forgiveness issues. Be prepared by committing time in prayer for your girls before class. (See Key to Success!)
      - Mention the Teel Relationship contract by Pam and Bill Farrel – a copy is provided on the Supplemental CD in Extra Helps folder
   b) Providing a note card, give the following instructions.
      1) Write a note to your father (or a well respected man who will bless them at their Celebration) telling him what they love and appreciate about him.
      2) Encourage the Daughters to invite this man to spend some time with them this week.

Keys to Success

In preparing some women to ask their father or step-in dad impart their blessing, un-forgiveness may become an issue. (As well as forgiveness in other relationships) Therefore, it is important to stress that un-forgiveness ends up hurting you instead of the person who has wronged you.

Encouraging those who want to forgive someone to write down the date they prayed and asked God to help them forgive that person.

Then emphasize that forgiveness is a process – it takes time. Their emotions will follow their act of faith, even if it takes awhile.

Note: Prepare invitations for distribution next week. Girls should tell you **today** how many they need.
A sample invitation is found in the **"Make It Your Own"** folder of the Supplemental CD

A Royal Touch

Depending on the ages represented in a group, sometimes it is worth dividing this lesson into two sessions:
- *The first session – Identifying a Man of Integrity*
- *The second session – Sexual Purity*
(Treasured Celebrations' highly recommends these DVD's
- *Pam Stenzel's Sex Has a Price Tag ,*
- *Lakita Garth's The Naked Truth. or you may have a similar DVD)*

* Don't worry – even if you divide Session 4 into two different sessions, you can still complete your program in 10 units. Session #6 is most often scheduled as a special evening event, so it can be done the same week/day as another unit.

A Royal Touch

Either the week of, or the week after, the discussion on Sexual Purity, I make a Purity Pledge certificate available to the girls – pointing out where they are, then letting them make the decision as to whether they would like to make that commitment or not. You don't want this to be an emotional or "people-pleasing" commitment, but a "heart-challenging, life-changing" one.

CD

* (This may be where you want to break up this into 2 different sessions, and show a video or have a guest speaker present a separate "Purity" topic)

7) Discuss sexual purity:
   a) What is sexual purity?
   b) Emphasize that when the Bible refers to sex it is a union between a couple.
   c) Sexual purity includes the body, soul <u>and</u> spirit.
   d) Show how their relationships with their fathers, boyfriends, and other men will affect their choice of a husband.
   e) Knowing your girls and how mature they are, think about encourage them to read the Book of Solomon – God's view of love and sex.

Whether you are doing this as one complete session or as two separate, emphasize the importance of meditating on the verse of the Session.

Psalm 15:2 (NIV paraphrased)
"Lord, who lives with You?
He who walks with integrity and speaks truth in his heart."

Leader's Notes:

Session 8:
The Princess
in the Mirror

Session 8 : <u>The Princess in the Mirror</u>

A Royal Touch

Sometimes I've placed a pile of my own journals that I have kept over the years as the centerpiece of the Presentation Table – stalking about the value of writing out our feelings.

Keys to Success

A guest speaker, a video, a song clip, etc. can make this session one of your most memorable – and valuable. We've used: <u>Growing in Perseverance DVD</u> (the Power of Prayer clip); Garth Brookes' song "Sometimes I Thank God for Unanswered Prayer"; Oswald Chamber's <u>My Utmost for His Highest</u> (October 11th entry) to name just a few – not to mention many fabulous guest speakers.

Note: Provide a video clip, a biography on a godly woman, *alive today,* OR the <u>live</u> testimonial from someone who has faced and overcome a significant challenge. Some suggestions would be a woman who has overcome an eating disorder, a physical disability, a sickness, the death of a loved one, abuse, or a series of difficult circumstances. This could be a popular personality or someone from your own congregation.

1) After viewing or sharing, discuss (or interview) how she must have *felt* and what she *chose* to do that enabled her to overcome and be a testimony to **faith**.

2) Discuss the following questions (from Day 1 of Chapter 8 in the BMDP journal):
   a) What is your definition of "feelings?"
      Webster defines "feelings" as: *mental perception (our own view of it); to have or obtain knowledge by the senses*
   b) Are our feelings always correct?
   c) What is your definition of "faith?"
      Webster defines "faith" as: *the agreeing in your mind to the truth of what is stated; a conviction to a system of religion; belief in something or someone*

3) Discuss the difference between Faith vs. Feelings.

4) Emphasize that God's definition of faith can be found in Hebrews 11:1: *"Faith is the assurance of things hoped for, the conviction of things not seen."*

5) Inform that the word "feelings" is used in the Bible only six times – but the word "faith" is referred to almost 600 times.

6) Ask the question, "Who do you know or have read about that you would consider a good example of a woman that didn't give in to her feelings and stood up for what was right?"
   a) Esther – Could she foresee that she was going to help save her people?
   b) Ruth – Could she foresee that she wouldn't be a widow forever , but would marry Boaz?

7) Encourage the girls to share a situation they may be facing and how this lesson might apply. Remind them that anything shared in their group together is private, confidential, and should never be shared with someone outside the class setting. Pray for each other!!

8) Prepare the Girls for the journaling they will do the next few days.
   a) Look thru Days 2-5 on pages 79-83 of the journal
   b) Encourage them to document "how they feel first thing in the morning" every day this week.
   c) Encourage them to think about the difference between "faith" and "feelings."
   d) Have them ask themselves whether they are going to respond to their situation by "walking in faith" or "acting on their feelings."
   e) Encourage them to document the outcome.
   f) If they give into their feelings vs. faith, encourage them to write how they could have responded differently.
   g) Point out the Mom or Mentor Moment and the project included at the end of Day 5.

9) Emphasize the importance of meditating on the verse of the week.

   "Every morning tell Him, thank You for Your kindness, and every evening rejoice in all His faithfulness." Psalm 92:2 (Living Bible

---

DISTRIBUTE CELEBRATION INVITATIONS!

Celebration should be scheduled by now, for at least 2-3 weeks from today, leaving room for 2 more sessions and a rehearsal. Give each girl an invitation she can photocopy, so she can distribute as many as she likes. (included on CD!)

Leader's Notes:

Session 9:

Dancing with The King

Session 9 : <u>Dancing with The King</u>

A Royal Touch

Your goal today is to create safety & intimacy for engaging, exploring, and expanding the most important relationship they can ever have.
You might light some candles put out some small chocolate treats, inexpensive gifts, or a beautiful vase of flowers.

Keys to Success

If your girls don't have a strong understanding of the foundations their faith, consider using something like the Apostles Creed to give them that foundation.

CD

A Royal Touch

Again, taking notes as the girls discover how they relate to God will give you a deeper understanding of them.
Use the bio sheet from the first session.

1) Have each Girl report on her journaling activity from last Session.

2) Discuss the following questions for the topic of this session:
   a) Describe how much God loves you?
   b) When do you spend time alone with God?
   c) How have you seen that reading God's Word will help you when you are hurting or troubled?
   d) When do you seek someone who knows God and talk with that person about God?
   e) What do you like about having God in your life?
   f) How do you think you can show God that you love Him?

3) Have the class break into two groups and document together things they see that affirm God's love for them using Psalm 103 and Romans 8:37-39. This is NOT in their journal, but they can use the blank page (pg. 84) that precedes Chapter 9 on pg. 85

4) Prepare the Girls for their last journal projects.
   a) Have them turn to Chapter 9, Day 3 on pg. 89 of their journals.
   b) Review "How I Relate to God" together, noticing their personality name from the first session together, then answer the question (on pg. 91 of journal):
      o Areas where I am strong in my relationship with God
      o Areas where I struggle
      o A personal commitment to make sure I find & value help in weaker areas of my walk with Him.

c) Remind them to be sure they go back and read from Day 1 and complete all the Days' project in their journals. Day 5 is an awesome opportunity to connect with their mothers/mentors .

Encourage them to finish strong on this last chapter!

5) Emphasize the importance of meditating on the verse of the week.

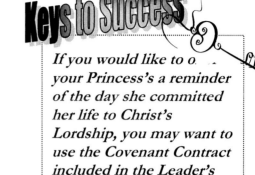

Keys to Success

If you would like to o.... your Princess's a reminder of the day she committed her life to Christ's Lordship, you may want to use the Covenant Contract included in the Leader's CD- Session Supplements section.

Jeremiah 29:11 (LB)
"For I know the plans that I have for you" declares the Lord, "plans for good and not for evil, to give you a future and a hope."**

A Royal Touch

Young people need to know that we adults struggle in our relationship with God, too! Don't be afraid to share your personal ups and downs in your Christian walk if the Lord leads you to.
You will be amazed at the level of intimacy and trust your openness can create.

Leader's Notes:

Session 10:

A Crowning Celebration

Session 10 : *A Crowning Celebration*

A Royal Touch

A simple but elegant centerpiece for your Presentation Table or a podium is as easy as finding a beautiful colored fabric and adding one elegant touch... Cover your table with the fabric and add a tiara to crown the day.

Keys to Success

Have the Celebration Biography sheets and Memories sheets printed out and ready before class.

CD

Keys to Success

Sometimes there will be a problem choosing favorite scriptures, so having a Strong's concordance with you this week will help. Have them look through their Journals for the scriptures they learned during the program, scriptures you may have used on gifts, or their favorite verse from Ps. 130 (Session 1) can help, too.

1) Allow time for the Girl's to share from their study over the last few days. What parts of the *"Dancing with the King"* chapter was especially meaningful to them.

2) Have each Girl complete a Biography sheet for you and collect them before they leave.

3) Make this the time where each Girl shares freely the following information with the class:
   a) Their favorite Bible verse.

   b) Why it is their favorite Bible verse.

   c) The benefits of attending the class.

   d) How attending the class has brought them to a greater understanding of themselves.

   e) How attending the class has brought them to a greater understanding of their relationship with God and/or with others in their lives.

4) Discuss their roles and responsibilities in the "Night of Celebration."
   a) Advise they will be expected to share their favorite Bible verse, and the reason it means so much to them.
   b) Ask them to chose their favorite session from the 9 preceding and be able to tell what it was that spoke to their hearts from that particular study.
   c) Emphasize that this activity will allow the audience to see each Girl's desire to live as godly young women, and give them an opportunity to speak publicly – a valuable and necessary skill to have as a Princess!!

5) Encourage each Girl to practice in front of each other. Give them the remainder of your time together to do so! This will help them to feel comfortable and confident when speaking at their Celebration.

6) Review & practice the agenda for the "Night of Celebration" (i.e. walking down the aisle to join their fathers in the front of your Celebration facility, what to do as they are introduced, where they will stand to receive their blessing, etc.)

7) Give each Girl a "Memories from My Celebration" sheet to help her document her special night.

Keys to Success

Before Celebration:
Letting all the girls do a complete walk thru of their Celebration before the actual event will help curb the nerves of your Princesses. Having them share in front of each other (before there is a whole room of strangers staring at them) is so valuable! It will really help those that haven't ever spoken in front of a group, and will give you a chance to help guide their thoughts and words, if need be.
*Remember – being able to speak in public is something a princess has to be able to do, too!

Keys to Success

After Celebration:
Give each Princess , her father (the man who blesses her), and her mother the appropriate Evaluation Sheet to complete and return to you. These are valuable tools that help you to evaluate areas where you can change, tailor, or otherwise enhance your Becoming A Modern Day Princess programs in the future.
Be sure to fill out your own evaluation, too!
(Found in the "Make It Your Own" section of the Supplemental CD)

CD

Leader's Notes:

CPSIA information can be obtained at www.ICGtesting.com
Printed in the USA
LVOW031737090312

272417LV00020B/11/P